LEADING WOMEN

Malala Yousafzai

Teenage
Education
Activist
Who Defied
the Taliban

CATHLEEN SMALL

Cavendish
Square
New York

To Sam, who inspires me in every way. You are changing the world, my son. Tiny but mighty!

Published in 2015 by Cavendish Square Publishing, LLC
243 5th Avenue, Suite 136, New York, NY 10016

First Edition

Website: cavendishsq.com

This publication represents the opinions and views of the author based on his or her personal experience, knowledge, and research. The information in this book serves as a general guide only. The author and publisher have used their best efforts in preparing this book and disclaim liability rising directly or indirectly from the use and application of this book.

CPSIA Compliance Information: Batch #WS14CSQ

All websites were available and accurate when this book was sent to press.

Library of Congress Cataloging-in-Publication Data

Small, Cathleen, author.
Malala Yousafzai : teenage education activist who defied the Taliban / Cathleen Small.
p. cm. — (Leading women)
Includes bibliographical references and index.
ISBN 978-1-62712-972-5 (hardcover) ISBN 978-1-62712-974-9 (ebook)
1. Yousafzai, Malala, 1997- 2. Girls—Education—Pakistan. 3. Sex discrimination in educa-tion—Pakistan. 4. Women social reformers—Pakistan—Biography. 5. Social reformers—Pakistan—Biography. 6. Political activists—Pakistan—Biography. 7. Girls—Violence against—Pakistan. I. Title.

LC2330.S63 2015
371.822095491—dc23

2014001536

Editorial Director: Dean Miller
Editor: Andrew Coddington
Senior Copy Editor: Wendy A. Reynolds
Art Director: Jeffrey Talbot
Designer: Amy Greenan/Joseph Macri
Photo Researcher: J8 Media
Production Manager: Jennifer Ryder-Talbot
Production Editor: David McNamara

Printed in the United States of America

CONTENTS

CHAPTER ONE

Life in Swat Before the Taliban

Malala Yousafzai is known by many as "the girl shot by the **Taliban**." Indeed, Malala *is* the Pakistani girl who, at the age of fifteen, survived a point-blank assassination attempt by the Taliban as she rode the bus home from school. However, that is not how Malala wishes to be known. Instead, she wants the world to know her as the "girl who fought for education." In any case, knowing where and from whom Malala came is essential to understanding who she is now.

Celebrating the Birth of a Daughter: A Father's Pride

Malala is from Pakistan, but she considers herself first and foremost a **Pashtun**. Pashtuns like Malala's family follow an unwritten ethical code that largely prizes a traditional lifestyle guided by ancient Islamic and Pashtunwali values of self-respect, tolerance, hospitality, love, forgiveness, and revenge. Male children grow up to be the providers in Pashtun society, as well as the decision-makers. A female child will grow up to be a woman whose primary purpose in life is to bear children and prepare food for the household. Thus, the birth of a boy is celebrated among Pashtuns, whereas the birth of a girl is reason for disappointment. Ziauddin Yousafzai, Malala's father, was unique among Pashtun men when he rejoiced upon discovering his first living child was a girl.

The Pashtun

The Pashtun people live in northeastern Afghanistan and northern Pakistan, near the Hindu Kush mountains. The majority of the Afghan population is Pashtun, as are many of the people in the Swat Valley. At the turn of the twenty-first century, roughly eleven million Pashtun lived in Afghanistan and twenty-five million lived in Pakistan. The Pashtun are a patriarchal society. Although hospitality and honor are of critical importance, bloody feuds between families and clans are common.

When Malala was born in a tiny two-room shack in the Swat Valley of Pakistan in 1997, her mother,

Tor Pekai, was disappointed, as the culture expects—but her father, Ziauddin, felt differently. Ziauddin and Tor Pekai's first child was stillborn, so when Malala was born kicking and screaming, her father fell instantly in love with the feisty child, saying,

"I know there is something different about this baby."

Although Pashtuns typically only trace the male lineage in families, Ziauddin drew an entry in his family tree for his newborn daughter, whom they named after Malala of Maiwand, an Afghani heroine known as the Afghan Joan of Arc. Ziauddin asked his friends to throw dried

Malala's brother takes a picture of her with a tablet while she addresses the United Nations.

fruit, sweets, and coins into his daughter's cradle, despite this ritual ordinarily being reserved for male children.

A Mother's Quiet Strength

Malala's mother, Tor Pekai, was a brown-haired beauty when Ziauddin Yousafzai met her. Marriages in Pashtun society are typically arranged, but this was not the case for Malala's parents. Although neither Ziauddin's nor Tor Pekai's family was pleased about the match, Ziauddin persisted and eventually married his beloved, after wooing her by sending her poems. Ironically, Tor Pekai couldn't read the poems he sent, as she had not attended much school. However, she fell in love with his intellect, and he admired her beauty.

In Pashtun society, women are secondary to men. They cook and raise the children, but they do not have a voice in most household decisions. In fact, it is considered a bit shameful for a Pashtun man to consult with his wife on important matters. However, Ziauddin was not a typical Pashtun man. He strongly valued Tor Pekai's opinion. He rarely made a major decision without consulting his wife first, despite the reaction this evoked in other Pashtun men. Furthermore, although spousal abuse is not uncommon in Pashtun culture, Ziauddin never laid a hand on Tor Pekai.

Although she is quiet, traditional, and so modest that she even refused to be photographed until very recently, Tor Pekai is a strong woman who comes from a family of strong women. She chose not to attend school herself, but she supported Malala's desire to get an education. A study in contrasts, Tor Pekai is very pious, prays regularly, and disapproves of dancing on religious grounds, yet she loves to shop and wears beautiful clothes and jewelry.

While Malala strongly identifies with her father, who shares her passion for education, her mother has also been a strong supporter and a source of Malala's strength. According to Malala, "My father always encouraged me to question him, but without my mother's support it would not have been possible for our family to continue fighting for what we believe in. She is my anchor."

Two Brothers Complete the Family

Although Ziauddin was delighted with his daughter, he was also pleased to welcome two sons to the family. Khushal, named after a Pashtun warrior and poet, was born when Malala was two, and was immediately the apple of their mother's eye. Malala, however, wasn't quite so enchanted by this new sibling, who had their mother wrapped around his tiny finger. To this day, the siblings disagree and quarrel, as so many brothers and sisters do.

The family was complete when another boy, Atal, joined them five years later. Most families in the Swat region have seven or eight children, but Ziauddin felt strongly that his family was complete with three.

Living in Mingora

Mingora is the largest city in the Swat Valley, which lies in northern Pakistan, just 100 miles (160 kilometers) from Islamabad, the country's capital. At 3,228 feet (984 meters) above sea level, Mingora is hardly the dry, dusty desert that is often associated with the Middle East. Rather, Mingora was once a major tourist destination and was considered by some to be the Switzerland of the Middle East, with its majestic mountains, colorful wildflowers, picturesque waterfalls, and sparkling lakes. In recent pre-Taliban years, however, Mingora became crowded and dirty due to an increase in population, unlike

A main street in Mingora. Recently, the population of Mingora has been increasing, leading to overcrowding.

The Taliban

The Taliban are a militant Islamic fundamentalist group. Originally, they suggested that Muslims had strayed from the teachings of the **Quran**, the central religious text of Islam, and would do well to return to their religious roots. However, to further their agenda, the Taliban turned to militant, bloody tactics, intent on gaining power mainly in Afghanistan and Pakistan. The Taliban is made up largely of Pashtuns, but by no means are all Pashtuns members of the Taliban.

the rest of the sparkling Swat Valley that surrounds it. Since the Taliban has moved into Mingora, it barely resembles the city of Malala's early years.

The Swat Valley is currently considered part of the Khyber Pakhtunkhwa province of Pakistan, but this is a relatively recent development. Prior to 1969, it was a **princely state,** separate from the rest of Pakistan and generally not under the Pakistani government. After 1969, the Pakistani government ruled Swat along with the rest of Pakistan, but since the arrival of the Taliban in the region, their control has been tenuous at best.

Malala's childhood home is in what used to be called the Butkara region, which means "place of the Buddhist statues." Swat had been a Buddhist kingdom for more than 500 years, before Islam became the predominant religion in the region in the eleventh century. Growing up, Malala and her brothers and friends played hide-and-seek amidst the ruins of Buddhist temples—rather ironic,

These ruins in the Butkara region near Mingora used to be part of an ancient Buddhist temple structure.

with the peace-loving philosophy of Buddhism being a striking contrast to the angry unrest and bloodshed that would take place in the region once the Taliban arrived.

Ziauddin Builds a School

Malala's father has always been passionate about education. Ziauddin grew up one of seven children in a primitive village called Barkana. The family of nine lived in a rundown one-story house with a leaky mud roof, but Ziauddin's father, Rohul Amin, was a powerful man. A high school theology teacher, he was also an influential, well-known public speaker in the region. It was a lot for young Ziauddin, who was afflicted with an embarrassing stutter, to live up to. Fiery-tempered Rohul Amin would yell at Ziauddin when he stuttered, which compounded the issue. Ziauddin combated the problem by entering a public-speaking competition at the age of thirteen. His teachers and friends tried to make young Ziauddin see how foolish the idea was, and Rohul Amin laughed out loud at the idea. But Ziauddin was determined and asked Rohul Amin to write his speech. "You write the speech and I will learn it," Ziauddin insisted. He memorized every word while walking in the hills near his home, and when the day of the competition arrived, a nervous Ziauddin delivered a flawless speech that made even Rohul Amin smile.

Ziauddin's love of words and speaking, as well as his thirst for knowledge, led to his desire to found a school. The primary occupations for males from his village were coal mining and construction, neither of which interested Ziauddin. For a while, he thought about being a **_jihadi_**, or religious warrior. He considered joining the same group that would later become the Swat Taliban, who were then fighting the Russians. However, Ziauddin was a questioner, not a follower. After meeting his future brother-in-law, Faiz Mohammad, who spoke of socialism and ending the feudal system in Pakistan, Ziauddin questioned what he was learning from the senior *talib* under whom he was studying jihad.

Ultimately, Ziauddin's decision to turn away from jihad may also have been influenced by his own father. Although he was a difficult man to please, Rohul Amin passed down to Ziauddin a love of learning and an awareness of human rights issues. In the end, the allure of jihad was no match for Ziauddin's belief in human rights and a better life for the Pashtun people. He returned to his dream of someday opening a school.

Ziauddin dreamed of a **madrasa** where all Pakistani children could receive an education despite gender or financial state. He wanted a school for all students—male and female, rich and poor—with desks, a library, computers, and bathrooms. Opening a school was no small endeavor, though. Ziauddin needed money and contacts, and he needed to go to college. Rohul Amin refused to pay for Ziauddin's living expenses while he studied, so even though Ziauddin had access to a free education at Jehanzeb College in Swat, he had no means to live while going to school. He hoped to live with his sister and brother-in-law while attending school, but his brother-in-law refused. Unable to find a solution to his problem, Ziauddin volunteered to help his uncle teach in a local school—and he got his lucky break. A man in the village where Ziauddin and his uncle were teaching offered to let Ziauddin live with him and his wife while attending Jehanzeb College. Ziauddin quickly and gratefully agreed.

> *Ziauddin dreamed of a place where all Pakistani children could receive an education, despite gender or financial state.*

Upon graduating from Jehanzeb College, Ziauddin worked as an English teacher at a private college. However, he was frustrated by the low pay and the school's strict curriculum, which did not encourage the sharing of opinions and a free exchange of independent thought. One of his colleagues, Naeem Khan, felt similarly, and the two men started a school in Mingora. The building they rented wasn't quite the dream school with modern, sparkling facilities that Ziauddin had had in mind. Rather, it was located next to a river where people threw their trash, and the odor was particularly noxious in warm weather. Still, it was a school, and it was Ziauddin's to do with as he and his partner pleased. Although it lacked plumbing or a kitchen, they then rented the shack across the road to live in, and began fixing up the school and looking for students.

Unfortunately, the two men were better friends than they were business partners, and tensions over the direction of the school soon arose. Their budget proved to be too small, and there were not as many interested students as the men had hoped. After three months, something had to be done. Ziauddin took on a new partner, Hidayatullah, an old college friend, who bought out Naeem and took his place. Together, the men named their endeavor the Khushal School, after a Pashtun warrior poet. Ziauddin would later give his first son the same name.

In the beginning, Khushal School had just three students and very little money. The men were also unable to officially register the school with the authorities, as the official of schools wanted a bribe that they couldn't afford. Ziauddin responded by joining the Swat Association of Private Schools and quickly becoming their vice president. He later became president of the association and grew it from fifteen members to 400. Now these school owners had some power, as there was strength in numbers. One man might not have much sway with the school authorities, but a group of 400 men was another story. However, money was still so tight that Ziauddin resorted to making snacks at night that they could sell to the children the next day, bringing in a bit more income.

When Ziauddin married Tor Pekai and brought her back to live with him in the two-room shack he now shared with Hidayatullah, finances got even tighter. For many months, Ziauddin and Hidayatullah couldn't afford to pay teachers' salaries or the rent for the school building. Eventually, Ziauddin had to sell Tor Pekai's wedding jewelry to bring in some money.

Things went from bad to worse when flash floods hit Mingora. The shack and the school were virtually destroyed by floodwaters, with everything caked in fetid mud. After a week spent cleaning up, a second flood hit the school ten days later.

Ziauddin finally felt his luck had changed on July 12, 1997, when he and Tor Pekai welcomed Malala to the world in their muddy shack. Just three months later, the family and Hidayatullah were able to move into a three-room apartment above the school—with running water. It was a small improvement, but an improvement nonetheless.

Khushal School was improving, too. By the time Malala was born, the school had about 100 students and five or six teachers. Ziauddin acted as principal, teacher, accountant, janitor, and maintenance man. His dream was coming true, if slowly. He even began to plan for a second school, which he intended to name the Malala Education Academy after his beloved daughter. However, Ziauddin and Hidayatullah began to find working together difficult. They eventually divided up their students and went their separate ways.

Since Malala lived above the school and her father was there all the time, she largely grew up in the classrooms, and was a great favorite with the students and teachers. According to Ziauddin, even before Malala could talk, she would "toddle into classes and talk as if [she] were a teacher." To Malala, the school was home. To Ziauddin, it was a dream come true.

CHAPTER TWO

The Taliban Moves In

Before the Taliban moved into the Swat Valley, Mingora was a bustling but pleasant place to live. Malala attended her father's school and played cricket with her brothers and the neighborhood children, all the while dreaming of a future in which she would be a doctor—one of few acceptable professions for Pashtun women. However, slowly and insidiously, the Taliban moved in and began to take over Mingora and the Swat Valley, and residents' lives changed. Some joined the Taliban, while others, like Malala and her family, quietly resisted while attempting to keep a relatively low profile.

Pakistani Law and How the Taliban Found a Way In

Historically speaking, whenever a militant or extremist group takes over a region, those on the outside look on in horror, wondering how it could've happened. Perhaps the most memorable example is the Holocaust. Many decades later, people look back and wonder how Hitler was ever allowed to take power. However, Hitler didn't simply announce one day that he planned to murder millions of Jews, Gypsies, homosexuals, and developmentally disabled persons and then take over much of central Europe. Such changes don't happen overnight.

Similarly, the Taliban didn't simply announce that they planned to take over Afghanistan and Pakistan and start murdering people. Instead, like any intelligent extremist group, they found an existing weakness and exploited it. In the case of the Swat Valley, a key weakness was the dissatisfaction many residents felt about living under Pakistani rule and law. Before 1969, Swatis had lived under their own Pashtun code; it was only after 1969 that the Swat Valley came under the control of the Pakistani government, a development that was distasteful to many Swatis. The Taliban saw their displeasure and promised them something better to gain their trust. What Swatis needed, the Taliban suggested, was a return to their religious roots and the teachings of the Quran. Dissatisfaction with the corrupt Pakistani government led many Swatis—including initially Malala's mother, Tor Pekai—to be open to the Taliban's message. And so the Taliban gained power slowly—just as Hitler had gradually gained power by promising the struggling German people economic prosperity.

Fazlullah, the Radio Mullah

Malala describes the Taliban coming to the Swat Valley almost overnight—a band of men with "long straggly hair and beards and camouflage vests over their *shalwar kamiz*… and sometimes stockings over their heads with holes for their eyes." Indeed, these men with their black badges proclaiming "*Sharia* **Law** or Martyrdom" did arrive rather abruptly. These men may have been part of the brute force of the Taliban, but they weren't necessarily the ubiquitous, persuasive voice of the Taliban that lured Swatis to consider the promise of another life. That voice belonged to Maulana Fazlullah.

Fazlullah was twenty-eight years old, a former pulley-chair operator afflicted by childhood polio and married to the daughter of Sufi Mohammad, a radical Islamist. Sufi Mohammad was the founder of *Tehrik-e-Nifaz-e-Sharia-e-Mohammadi*, or the Movement for the Enforcement of Islamic Law (**TNSM**). Fazlullah didn't come in with a frightening demeanor or a "Sharia Law or Martyrdom" badge like the men who came down from Upper Swat. Instead, he appealed to the Swatis' devotion to the Quran. He called himself an "Islamic reformer and interpreter of the Quran," and used an illegal radio station to encourage Swatis to adopt positive practices and avoid negative ones. For example, he told the Swati men to quit using drugs such as heroin and hashish. He also urged them to keep their beards, and wash their body parts in a specified order. All of these declarations, Fazlullah claimed, were in the teachings of the Quran. Since Swatis are a largely devout people who try to follow the Quran, they were open to Fazlullah's teachings.

Maulana Fazlullah, circa 2008.

The problem, as Malala saw it, was that many Swatis could not read the original Arabic of the Quran, and thus were subject to misinterpretations of it by *mullahs* such as Fazlullah. Malala, however, had not only finished her recitation of the complete Quran, she had also started learning to translate the original Arabic of the text. Doing so allowed her to recognize when mullahs like Fazlullah were putting forth misinterpretations of the text.

Fazlullah also gained power in the remote areas of the Swat Valley, which had been hit hard by a 7.6-magnitude earthquake in 2005. The government hadn't offered quake victims much help, but the TNSM had stepped in with volunteers. Fazlullah gained a following among the poorer people of the region, who saw him as a sort of Robin Hood figure because of his criticism of the feudal system in Pakistan.

Fazlullah was charismatic, and many Swatis liked what he had to say about bringing back Islamic law. Fed up with the Pakistani legal system and its corruption, many Swatis felt that Fazlullah's idea of bringing back Islamic law would return them to the glory days before 1969, when the **wali** were in power. It wasn't until later, when Fazlullah set up a kind of local court called a shura, that people began to learn that the Taliban's idea of law was quite brutal. Fazlullah's punishments often included public whippings—and worse.

A butcher is publicly whipped by the Taliban in Swat. He was charged with selling meat from animals that were slaughtered without following proper Muslim procedure.

Ziauddin's friend and former business partner, Hidayatullah, summed up Fazlullah's rise to power well:

> "This is how these militants work. They want to win the hearts and minds of the people, so they first see what the local problems are and target those responsible, and that way they get the support of the silent majority... After, when they get power, they behave like the criminals they once hunted down."

Ziauddin agreed, saying that "people had been seduced by Fazlullah." One such group were the manual workers in the Swat Valley. Manual laborers weren't well thought of in the Pashtun culture of the area, and many joined the Taliban to try to achieve some level of status and power.

Fazlullah often aimed his ideas at women. He told them to stay inside the house, fulfill their homemaker duties, and only go outside in emergencies—and then, only when covered by a veil. The mothers of many of her friends took Fazlullah's teachings to heart, but Malala found them confusing. She was aware that nowhere in the Quran is it written that men should be the only ones to go outside. In fact, despite being very devout and interested in Fazlullah's teachings, Malala's own mother, Tor Pekai, was a strong woman who had a fairly active role in running the family's life—she wasn't hiding in the house. Malala therefore questioned what she heard, and Ziauddin, who was horrified by Fazlullah's teachings, encouraged her to do so.

Eventually, many of those who had initially followed Fazlullah, and felt him to be a good interpreter of the Quran, began to question his teachings as they became more extreme. But by then, it was too late—the Taliban had come to Swat, and getting them out would not be easy.

Threats to Ziauddin's School

Since the Taliban believed that women should be solely in the home, Khushal School naturally came under fire, particularly after Sufi Mohammad issued a proclamation from jail, where he was imprisoned for being a militant leader, that girls should not be educated. According to the Taliban, educating women was against the Quran (another "teaching" that Malala knew was not stated anywhere in the Quran). At first, the reach of the Taliban into the school was relatively minor—an Urdu teacher took a day off work to help build a headquarters for Fazlullah, and shortly thereafter told Ziauddin that he could no longer teach girls because Fazlullah didn't like it. Then a second teacher refused to teach girls as well.

Not long after, a letter taped to the Khushal School gates proclaimed:

> *Sir, the school you are running is Western and infidel. You teach girls and have a uniform that is un-Islamic. Stop this, or you will be in trouble and your children will weep and cry for you.*
>
> *~Fedayeen of Islam [translation: Devotees of Islam, or Islamic sacrificers]*

Ziauddin answered the threat by changing the boys' uniform to a more traditional shalwar kamiz. He did not change the girls' uniform, but he did advise his female students to keep their heads covered while coming into and going out of school.

Female students at school in Mingora. As the Taliban moved into the Swat Valley, girls had to keep their heads covered while travelling to and from school.

Fazlullah also outlawed school field trips, which Malala and her fellow students had once enjoyed, because girls were not to be seen outside.

Attending School in Secret

Eventually, the girls attending Khushal School had to stop wearing uniforms altogether, lest they encounter a Taliban member on their way to school. They hid their books and schoolbags with their shawls as they walked swiftly to the building, which no longer even had a sign out front. This troubled Malala, but she was happy for any chance to go to school, even if it meant doing so in secret.

Inside the school walls, away from the prying eyes of the Taliban, it was largely business as usual for Malala. Competitive by nature, she was forever striving to be at the top of her class. It was around this time that Malala changed her career aspirations. Instead of being a doctor, she decided she wanted to become an inventor and make "an anti-Taliban machine which would sniff them out and destroy their guns." Little wonder, given that in early 2008, the Taliban had begun to blow up schools—though at least they usually did so at night when no students were present. This wasn't always the case, though. In one instance, a Taliban suicide bomber hit Haji Baba High School in Mingora while a funeral service was going on. More than fifty-five people were killed. The Taliban were moving ever closer, invading the safe haven that schools had once provided. By late 2008, the Taliban had destroyed approximately 400 schools.

Khushal School continued to operate, but most of the girls no longer attended. Malala's class, which had twenty-seven female students prior to the ban, was down to ten girls. Some females had left the area to continue their education in Peshawar, but Ziauddin held firm in his desire to stay in the Swat Valley, with his school. Thus, Malala stayed on as a pupil, albeit in secret.

At the end of 2008, Fazlullah decreed that all girls' schools would close as of January 15, 2009. Eleven-year-old Malala was devastated; her pain was documented by filmmaker Adam Ellick and Pakistani journalist Irfan Ashraf in a now-famous 2009 documentary, *Class Dismissed in Swat Valley*. Further establishing herself as an activist for education, Malala told Ellick and Ashraf,

> *"They cannot stop me. I will get my education if it's at home, school, or somewhere else. This is our request to the world—to save our schools, save our Pakistan, save our Swat."*

Unfortunately, Malala's request fell on the deaf ears of the Taliban, who destroyed five more schools in the four days after the ban on girls' schools began. However, there was a bit of hope when journalist Abdul Hai Kakar engaged in secret talks with Fazlullah and pressured him to reconsider his ban on girls' education, citing backlash from the Pakistani people. Fazlullah agreed to lift the ban, but only for girls up to ten years old. Eleven-year-old Malala and some of her friends pretended they were younger and returned to school—again, in secret. The punishment for doing so could be flogging or death, yet Malala went, because education was that important to her.

CHAPTER THREE

The Beginnings of Activism

By 2007, the Taliban was officially in the Swat Valley. Schools that dared to educate girls were a big target, but certainly not the only target. Maulana Fazlullah and the Swat Taliban wanted to impose extreme sharia law and the associated punishments they deemed fair, and almost everyone was a target. As a young female, Malala might have been safe from their wrath—if she hadn't decided to stand up for education rights.

Living Under the Taliban

Under the Taliban, Swatis were forced to live in an even more traditional, male-dominated society than they had under the Pashtun way of life. Swati women had long been primarily homemakers, but before the Taliban's arrival they had been allowed to go out in typical Pashtun dress and visit local bazaars and shops. Once the Taliban took over, women were told to stay home and only venture out in emergencies. Even in those situations, they were told to wear *burqas* to cover their faces.

These women are following the Taliban law that requires women to wear burqas covering their faces whenever they leave the house.

Other than their interpretation of the Quran, nothing was sacred to the Swat Taliban. In the Butkara region in Mingora where Malala and her family lived, the remains of old Buddhist temples and statues were everywhere, an important reminder of Swat's history as a one-time

Buddhist kingdom. However, the Taliban believed statues and paintings to be sinful, so they destroyed the remains. As Malala describes,

> *"The Taliban became the enemy of fine arts, culture, and our history."*

Perhaps most notably, the Swat Taliban destroyed a twenty-three-foot Buddha that was carved into a hillside near Mingora. The carving had watched over the valley for fifteen centuries, but the Taliban destroyed it without a second thought.

Worse than the destruction of Swati history, though, was the painful destruction of its people. When the Taliban moved in and began killing, they did so ceaselessly. Even the police were not immune. The Taliban had assassinated several police officers, so now the police would flee whenever Taliban soldiers moved in to take over villages. As Malala recounts, "Policemen were so scared of being killed that they took out ads in the newspapers to announce they had left the force."

Things were rapidly going from bad to worse in the Swat Valley. Maulana Fazlullah declared war on the Pakistani government. Murders were happening with alarming frequency and growing ever closer to Mingora, which had previously been safer than the outlying areas of the Swat Valley. The Pakistani army moved into

Benazir Bhutto, circa 2007.

Mingora in the fall of 2007 and established a curfew for residents. In late October 2007, the army claimed to have killed more than a hundred members of the Taliban, but on November 1st, 700 Taliban soldiers took over a Pakistani army post at Khwazakhela, and then quickly overran police stations there and in Madyan. It was one step forward and two steps back for the Pakistani army, who would make some progress against the Taliban, only to have the Taliban gain more ground and take over more of the region. Within weeks, the Taliban had taken control of most of Swat outside of Mingora.

The Taliban flaunted their brutal rule. People went to watch public floggings, which were announced by Radio Mullah. Victims' bodies were dumped for everyone to

Benazir Bhutto: Pakistan's Hope for Peace

Malala and her fellow Swatis felt a brief glimmer of hope when Benazir Bhutto returned to Pakistan. Bhutto was Pakistan's first (and so far, only) female prime minister, but she had gone into exile in 1999 after being dismissed on corruption charges. However, in 2007, the unpopular General Musharraf was in power in Pakistan. Concerned that his unpopularity would render him ineffective against the Taliban, the American government helped facilitate an agreement whereby Musharraf would act as civilian president, grant amnesty to Bhutto, and be supported by her well-liked political party.

As Malala recalls, Benazir Bhutto was a role model for Pakistani girls. She symbolized democracy and hope to the struggling nation, and it was because of her that they could dream of being heard and becoming politicians. Perhaps not surprisingly, an assassination attempt was made right away. Her first day back in Pakistan, Bhutto was the target of a bombing. Despite surviving this first attempt, Bhutto was assassinated barely two months later, on December 27, 2007.

see in what became known as the Bloody Square. The Taliban often pinned threatening notes to the bodies, warning Swatis that they could be next. One such victim was Shabana, a celebrated Swati dancer and dance teacher, who was killed because Taliban consider dancing to be immoral. A teacher was also killed when he refused to pull his shalwar kamiz above his ankle, stating that nowhere in Islam is that a requirement of dress. He was hanged and his father was shot for this seemingly minor transgression.

The Taliban were not the only ones contributing to the violence in Peshawar. Here, police beat a man while breaking up a pro-Taliban demonstration.

The reach of the Taliban penetrated the safety of Malala's home. Ziauddin regularly slept at friends' houses in case the Taliban were to come for him in retaliation for his increasing outspokenness. He did not want to be killed in front of his family. Tor Pekai debated sleeping with a knife under her pillow. Malala's youngest brother, Atal, began digging a grave in the garden, in case the family was to need it. Malala and her family went to bed every night to the sounds of gunfire in the hills. Death was all around.

Speaking Out Against the Taliban

Distressed by the horrors occurring right outside her home, Malala looked to her father and her teachers to make sense of things. Ziauddin wasn't a man to sit back quietly; he openly discussed his distaste for the Taliban and his belief that girls deserved an education, despite others warning him that he was risking his life by doing so. In fact, Malala often went with Ziauddin when he met up with his fellow activists, who considered her "not just the daughter of Ziauddin… the daughter of all of us." Malala's beloved teacher, Madame Maryam, also encouraged her to continue her studies despite the danger.

With these influences and the example of Benazir Bhutto to look up to, Malala began to venture into the world of activism. However, it was Bhutto's assassination in December 2007 that really pushed her into the role she would later fill: a strong voice for Pakistani girls.

Upon seeing the coverage of Bhutto's assassination on the news, Malala said,

> "[M]y heart said to me, Why don't you go there and fight for women's rights?"

Eleven-year-old Malala began to give interviews about girls and education in Pakistan—first as part of a group of students, but later on her own. Malala described her thoughts when she went on Geo, the largest news channel in Pakistan:

> "The media needs interviews. They want to interview a small girl, but the girls are scared, and even if they're not, their parents won't allow it. I have a father who isn't scared, who stands by me. He said, 'You are a child and it's your right to speak.'"

Malala's confidence grew as she did more interviews. She pondered,

> "If one man, Fazlullah, can destroy everything, why can't one girl change it?"

Gul Makai: BBC Blogger

As it turned out, Malala was about to become more visible than ever—while trying to remain invisible. Ziauddin was friends with a BBC radio correspondent in Peshawar, Abdul Hai Kakar, who was looking for a female teacher or student to write a diary about living under the Taliban. Hearing of this, Malala immediately volunteered. With her family's support, she began blogging for the BBC under the pseudonym of Gul Makai, the name of a heroine in a Pashtun folktale.

Protecting Malala's safety was paramount, so Hai Kakar took down her blogs over the phone. He even used his wife's phone, as he suspected his was bugged by intelligence services. Malala and Hai Kakar would speak in Urdu for thirty to forty-five minutes, with him asking her to tell him stories or answer questions about her day. Malala was a modern-day Anne Frank, and once a week her blogs appeared on the BBC Urdu website.

Malala's first blog entry was published on January 3, 2009, and was titled, "I Am Afraid." It was a fitting title, as Malala speaks of being on her way home from school and hearing a man say, "I will kill you." She later realizes that he must've been threatening someone on the phone and not her, but it is a stark portrayal of the terror Malala and her fellow female students endured just to engage in their basic human right to attend school.

In short order, Malala's blog gained attention outside of just the BBC Urdu site. Extracts were printed in newspapers, and the BBC made an audio recording of a girl reading it. As Malala recounts, "I began to see that the pen and the words that come from it can be much more powerful than machine guns, tanks, or helicopters."

Class Dismissed: Malala as a Documentary Subject

Less than two weeks after Malala began blogging as Gul Makai, she earned a chance for further exposure when she became the subject of a short documentary, *Class Dismissed in Swat Valley*, made by American journalist Adam Ellick and Pakistani journalist Irfan Ashraf. The documentary was to be shown on the *New York Times'* website, and was originally set to follow Ziauddin on the last day of school before the Taliban's ban on girls' schools went into effect on January 15, 2009. Malala sat with Ziauddin as the filmmakers interviewed him. Suddenly, Ashraf asked her, "What would you do if there comes a day when you can't go back to your valley and school?" Malala began to weep, and the focus of the documentary shifted to her. The filmmakers followed her as she prepared for her last morning of school and documented the events as she went to Khushal School and its special assembly that day.

The powerful twelve-minute documentary appeared on the *New York Times'* website on February 22, 2009, and gave a face to the youngest victims of the Swat Taliban: young girls whose right to education was being stripped away due to misinterpretation of the Quran. Ellick and Ashraf would later post a longer thirty-two-minute version, entitled *Class Dismissed: Malala's Story*, to the website on October 9, 2012—after an assassin's bullet almost silenced her forever.

Peace... or State-Sanctioned Terrorism?

In mid-February 2009, two years after the Taliban infiltrated the Swat Valley, a peace deal was supposedly struck between the **Awami National Party** (**ANP**) and the Taliban. The ANP agreed to impose sharia law in Swat if the Taliban would stop fighting. The Taliban agreed to a ten-day truce.

The deal somewhat defied logic: The Taliban's interpretation of sharia law was extreme and violent, and many—including Pakistan's American allies—wondered why the government would agree to such a thing. Then–Secretary of State Hillary Clinton commented, "I think the Pakistan government is basically abdicating to the Taliban and the extremists." However, the government hoped that by giving the Taliban what they wanted—sharia law as the region's legal system—the Taliban would then live peacefully.

Perhaps not surprisingly, this strategy backfired miserably. Despite the enactment of a supposed "permanent ceasefire" on February 22, 2009, the Taliban continued to kill, slaughtering a well-known TV reporter covering a peace march. Malala remembers that, "to our horror things didn't change much [under the ceasefire]. If anything, the Taliban became even more barbaric. They were now state-sanctioned terrorists... The peace deal was merely a mirage."

The outside world was beginning to get an idea of the Taliban's brutality, too. A viral video of a teenage girl being flogged thirty-four times by the Taliban in front of spectators who did nothing to help made the rounds on the Internet and sparked outrage. The girl's offense? Coming outside of her house with a man who was not her husband. Malala recalls being surprised by how upset people were over the video, as such incidents were fairly common in the Swat Valley. Clearly, outsiders had no idea what was really going on.

More troubling still was the fact that Pakistani officials were turning a blind eye to the Taliban. Zahid Hussain, a journalist, paid a visit to Deputy Commissioner Syed Javid, who had previously announced the permanent ceasefire. Hussain found the official hosting a celebration of the Taliban takeover. A number of senior Taliban commanders were in attendance, including one who had a bounty of $200,000 on his head. These types of incidents made Swatis wonder who was really in charge—the Pakistani government or the Taliban.

Sufi Mohammad, Maulana Fazlullah's father-in-law, had been released from prison and was said to be in favor of the peace deal. He had guaranteed the Swatis that the Taliban would cease killing and that peace would be restored to the Swat Valley. However, when April 20, 2009, arrived—the day that Sufi Mohammad was to address the Swatis and talk about the plans for peace—it became painfully apparent that, just as many had suspected, the peace deal was a mirage. He essentially threatened Pakistan as a whole, proclaiming, "I consider

The Taliban required people to destroy CDs and DVDs, which they considered sinful vices.

Western democracy a system imposed on us by the infidels. Islam does not allow democracy or elections... Now wait, we are coming to Islamabad!"

The Taliban invaded Buner, next to Swat and not far from Islamabad, and the police fled. The Taliban quickly and efficiently took over Buner and set up shariat courts. They also burned TVs, DVDs, and art on the grounds that such things were sinful.

Leaving Swat

In May 2009, the Pakistani army launched Operation True Path, in the hopes of driving the Taliban out of the Swat Valley. Residents of Mingora were urged to leave. While Ziauddin maintained that his family should stay, Tor Pekai prevailed. A family friend had lost a relative due to the ever-present violence, and Malala's mother put her foot down, telling Ziauddin, "You don't have to come, but I am going and I will take the children to Shangla." Ziauddin relented, and on May 5, 2009, Malala and her family left Mingora and became internally displaced persons, or IDPs.

They were not alone. The streets were full of people fleeing the battleground that the Swat Valley had become. People could bring very little with them, and many fled with only the clothes they were wearing. Almost a million people left, and as Malala recalls, it was the "biggest exodus in Pashtun history."

Refugees at Nasir Bagh Camp
in Pakistan.

Refugee camps were set up in Mardan, a busy city outside of the Swat Valley, but the camps were hot and filled with disease. It was rumored that there were Talibs hiding in the camps, too. Fortunately for many, Pashtun culture prizes hospitality, so a great many Swat IDPs were offered lodging by residents of Mardan and nearby Swabi.

Malala's family planned to stay with relatives in Shangla. They stopped in Mardan, where they spent one night with the friend who had given them a ride. There, Ziauddin departed and went to Peshawar, hoping to raise awareness about the conditions in which the refugees were living. Tor Pekai and the children bid him a worried goodbye and continued their journey to Shangla. They got a ride to the city of Besham, but were forced to walk the over fifteen miles (25 km) to Shangla, carrying all of their belongings.

They finally reached Tor Pekai's village and stayed with Malala's uncle, Faiz Mohammad—the same man who, years earlier, had befriended Ziauddin and encouraged him not to join the jihad. Malala missed her home, but was happy to be able to go to school with her cousin. It was a tiny school and more traditional than Khushal School (few girls attended, and those who did covered their faces and did not speak in public), but it was better than nothing, and Malala was relieved to return to her studies.

Tor Pekai and her children spent six weeks in Shangla before they got word from Ziauddin that they should travel to Peshawar. After an emotional reunion, the family traveled to Islamabad, where they stayed with an acquaintance. Twelve-year-old Malala did a radio interview while in Islamabad, and the station offered the family the chance to stay in a guesthouse in Abbottabad, the city where Osama bin Laden was eventually killed after hiding essentially in plain sight. Finally, they headed to Haripur, their fourth residence in two months. Malala appreciated not being in a refugee camp, but still missed her beloved Swat Valley. She wondered whether they would ever be able to return to their home.

CHAPTER FOUR

An Attempted Assassination

After Malala and her family had been away from Mingora for almost three months, they were finally able to return home. On July 24, 2009, the prime minister of Pakistan declared that the Taliban had been driven out of the Swat Valley, and encouraged residents to return. Although delighted to be able to go home, Malala and her family did so somewhat uneasily, wondering whether the Taliban was *really* gone.

A Return to Swat

The Swat Valley was supposedly under military control, with security checkpoints everywhere. Mingora was almost unrecognizable to what it had been—buildings used as hideouts by the Taliban had been blown up, and almost every building was riddled with bullet holes. Shops had been looted or shuttered, and every place was deserted. Mingora was like a ghost town, but at least the Taliban appeared to be gone.

Malala's home was largely intact. It had not been robbed, but the family's pet chickens had starved to death, and their remains lay in the overgrown garden. Khushal School was intact, though it had been used by the Pakistani army and was a mess of rotting food, cigarette butts, and graffiti.

Malala worried that the Taliban would return, despite the army's assurances that they had been driven out of the region. Fazlullah wasn't in custody, nor were many other senior members of the Taliban, so Malala and her family resumed life in Mingora with a sense of unease. Malala returned to school and public speaking. Festivals and music returned to the valley as well. But the specter of the Taliban lurked, ever present.

That specter grew more evident in November 2009, when a friend of Ziauddin's, also an outspoken critic of the Taliban, was ambushed as he returned home from a meeting. He escaped, but narrowly. And on December 1, 2009, a well-known ANP politician was killed by a suicide bomber near where Fazlullah's headquarters had been before the Pakistani army destroyed it.

Hard times weren't over for the residents of the valley, despite the apparent lack of the Taliban in the region. Monsoons hit Swat in July 2010, and the mountains, which the Taliban and timber smugglers had stripped of trees, couldn't handle the heavy rain, nor could the swollen rivers. Floodwaters covered the Swat Valley and other parts of Pakistan, and when it was over, approximately 2,000 people had drowned, and fourteen million people had been affected. Seven thousand schools were destroyed, and millions of people lost their homes. The devastation was tremendous, and Swat was one of the most heavily affected regions.

In 2010, monsoons flooded much of Swat, killing thousands and affecting millions more.

Volunteers from Islamic groups were among the first to lend a hand to the Swatis, all the while saying that the floods were God's punishment for the Swatis having enjoyed recent music and dancing. Both the Pakistani army and the American military lent aid as well. However, less foreign aid than usual was provided: agencies worried about the safety of their staff, since the Taliban had announced that Pakistan should reject any help from Christians or Jews. Given that the Taliban had bombed the World Food Program office in Islamabad less than a year prior, foreign aid agencies were leery of getting involved. The Taliban had also kidnapped and murdered three foreign aid workers from a Christian group, and had blown up two more schools. The vice chancellor of Swat University, who was an outspoken anti-Taliban Islamic scholar, was gunned down in his office. It was now apparent that the Taliban had never really left the region. They were simply regrouping and biding their time.

An Uneasy Peace—and a Young Advocate

By now Malala was thirteen years old, back in Mingora, and attending school once again. The Swat Valley was supposedly under the control of the Pakistani government, but at times that seemed like a minor improvement over the reign of the Taliban. Violence was still occurring on a regular basis, only now it was sometimes at the hands of the Pakistani military. Hundreds of Swatis were missing, and no one knew why, but many connected the disappearances to the army.

Some laws enacted under the Taliban's Islamization campaign were still in effect, too. Just because the Taliban no longer ruled the region, that didn't mean their rules weren't still in effect. In late 2010, a Christian woman in the region was sentenced to death for speaking favorably of Christ and questioning the Prophet Mohammad. After speaking on the woman's behalf and suggesting that she should be pardoned, Salman Taseer, the Pakistani governor of the Punjab region, was shot twenty-six times and killed. Perhaps even more shocking is the fact that Taseer's killer was widely praised and showered with rose petals in court. The region was supposedly free of the Taliban, but Malala wondered whether the people were really much better off. The activist continued to speak publicly about her views, advocating for education for every girl in Swat, as well as for street children and those working as child labor.

Malala was becoming well known for her advocacy. No longer did she have to hide behind the pen name Gul Makai. She was now speaking as Malala, and she was attracting attention. Archbishop Desmond Tutu from South Africa nominated her for the international peace prize of KidsRights, an Amsterdam-based children's advocacy group. She didn't win that prize, but she did receive Pakistan's first National Peace Prize. It was soon dubbed the Malala Prize, and would be awarded each year after to a child under eighteen years old, in Malala's honor.

Supporters of Salman Taseer's killer, Malik Mumtaz Qadri, hold a rally in Qadri's honor.

At the December 20, 2011, ceremony at the prime minister's official residence, Malala graciously received her award and a check from the prime minister—and then promptly gave him a list of demands! Among them, she wanted their schools rebuilt in Swat, as well as a girls' university built. Malala knew the prime minister wouldn't likely follow through on her demands, but she reflected,

> *"One day, I will be a politician and do these things myself."*

Malala Is Targeted

In January 2012, Malala, Ziauddin, Tor Pekai, and Atal traveled to the port city of Karachi, Pakistan, for Malala to be honored with the renaming of a girls' secondary school. The family attended the assembly honoring Malala, and stayed to visit some family and do a bit of sightseeing. While there, a Pakistani journalist named Shehla Anjum came to their hostel to meet Malala, whom she had seen in the *Class Dismissed* documentary on the *New York Times'* website. With tears in her eyes, Shehla asked Ziauddin whether he was aware that the Taliban had issued a threat against Malala. It was the first the family had heard about it.

Shehla got on the Internet and showed the family that the Taliban had just issued threats against Malala and another woman, an activist in Dir. The threat said, "These two are spreading secularism and should be killed." Malala didn't take the threat seriously, as the Taliban didn't typically target children and she was distrustful of the Internet source. However, when the family found out the police were looking to question them about whether they had received any threats, Ziauddin and Tor Pekai began to worry. Malala, however, took it in stride. As she recounts,

"It seemed to me that everyone knows they will die one day. My feeling was nobody can stop death; it doesn't matter if it comes from a Talib or cancer. So I should do whatever I want to do."

Ziauddin encouraged Malala to take the threat more seriously, suggesting that perhaps they should stop their activism for a while. Malala disagreed, telling Ziauddin, "You were the one who said if we believe in something greater than our lives, then our voices will only multiply even if we are dead. We can't disown our campaign!"

When the family returned to Swat, the police verified the threats and offered Malala and her family protection in the form of bodyguards. Ziauddin refused, given that many Swatis had been killed despite having bodyguards. He also felt the presence of the guards would alarm the parents of the Khushal School students, and perhaps put other students at risk.

Indeed, the peace in Swat was an uneasy one for Malala and her family. As Malala pointed out to Ziauddin,

"When there was Talibanization we were safe; now there are no Taliban we are unsafe."

A Threat Is Carried Out

As 2012 wore on, Malala and her family lived with the persistent reminder that they weren't truly safe. Members from intelligence services periodically showed up at their house to ask questions about the family, and Khushal School became the victim of negative propaganda when an anonymous person distributed letters and put up posters proclaiming that the school was "a center of vulgarity and obscenity."

In August, Ziauddin received more troubling news. His friend and fellow activist, Zahid Khan, had been shot in the face on his way to prayers at the mosque near his house. Miraculously, Zahid survived being shot at point-blank range, but Zahid and Ziauddin had been thought to be together on the Taliban radar, and Ziauddin was certain he would be the next target. However, he once again refused protection from the police, believing that if he were to be killed, it would be best if he were killed alone.

Given the increase in violence and the threats against Malala, Tor Pekai insisted that Malala take the bus home from school—despite it being only a five-minute walk. Even Malala began to take the threats more seriously. She lived in fear of being ambushed by the Taliban or having them throw acid in her face, as had been the fate of women in Afghanistan. At night, when everyone in her family was asleep, Malala would check every door and window, as well as the front gate, to make sure they were locked. However, she kept her curtains open at night, despite Ziauddin's urging to the contrary, because she wanted to be able to see everything.

She prayed. Ironically, many non-Taliban Muslims like Malala and her family, who the Taliban believe to be blasphemers who don't follow the Quran, actually believe fervently in God. Malala trusted God to protect her and prayed every night,

> *"Bless us. First our father and family, then our street, then our whole* **mohalla***, then all Swat. No, all Muslims. No, not just Muslims; bless all human beings."*

Malala prayed even more than usual in early October 2012, as it was exam time. She took her physics exam on October 8 and then stayed up late studying for her Pakistani studies exam, which she feared would be difficult for her. The next morning, Ziauddin and Tor Pekai woke Malala early, and Tor Pekai made her usual breakfast. Malala ate with her whole family. It wasn't just a big day for Malala. It was also a big day for Tor Pekai, who was to begin reading and writing lessons.

Malala was pleased to find that her Pakistani studies exam went well. She chatted with her friends while waiting for the bus home. When the bus arrived, Malala sat near the open back of the *dyna* with her best friend, Moniba. She liked to be able to see through the thick plastic sheeting that covered the sides of the bus.

That day, the usually busy road home seemed quiet and rather empty, and Malala asked Moniba, "Where are all the people?" Just then, two young men stepped out into the road and stopped the dyna. At first, Moniba thought the young man approaching the back of the dyna was another journalist coming to ask Malala for an interview—a fairly common occurrence. The young, bearded man was wearing a cap, his nose and mouth covered with a handkerchief. He leaned into the back of the dyna and demanded, "Who is Malala?" No one replied, but Malala was the only girl whose face was uncovered, and several of her classmates looked at her. That was all the proof the man needed. He fired three shots from a Colt .45 at point-blank range. The first bullet pierced Malala's left eye socket, and the bullet exited below her left shoulder. Malala slumped onto Moniba's lap, so the assassin's second and third bullets hit girls next to Malala in the hand and shoulder.

The last thing Malala remembers is thinking about the revision she needed to do for her exam the next day.

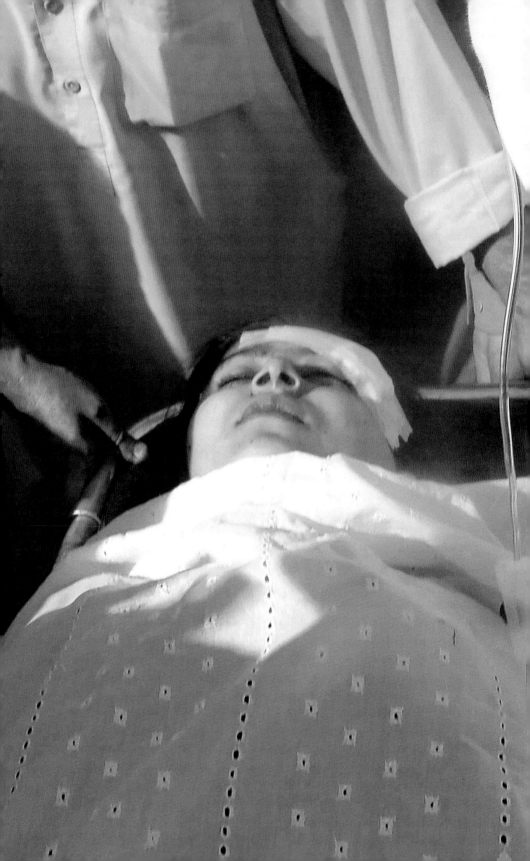

CHAPTER FIVE

Recovery

When two members of the Taliban stopped the dyna in which Malala was riding home from school, what happened next was almost unimaginable. The Taliban had the blood of many children and teens on its collective hands, but mainly those victims were innocent bystanders killed in bombings or suicide attacks. The Taliban didn't typically target children for assassination. However, Malala was no typical teenager, and the attempt on her life was swift and calculated.

Fortunately, the dyna's driver, Usman Bhai Jan, reacted equally swiftly and drove Malala and her classmates to Swat Central Hospital as quickly as possible. There, Malala's journey back to life began.

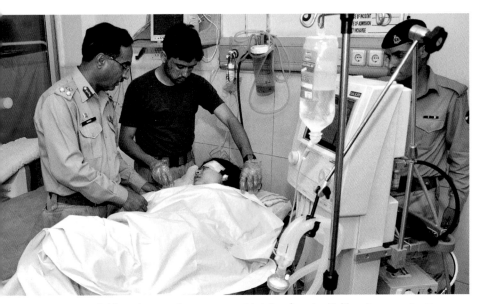

Pakistani army doctors treat Malala after the Taliban's assassination attempt.

Swat Central Hospital

Ziauddin was about to give a speech to four hundred principals from the Association of Private Schools when he received word that shots had been fired in the vicinity of Khushal School's dyna. Having no idea that any students had been shot but aware that his daughter rode the dyna home from school, Ziauddin gave his speech as planned—but his concern was enough that he rushed off the stage without taking questions after his speech, and sped to Swat Central Hospital. When he saw the crowds, photographers, and TV cameras outside the hospital, Ziauddin knew his worst fear had come true—Malala had been hurt. He kissed his daughter as she lay on a gurney, her eyes closed.

The initial news from the doctors was promising—
a computed tomography, or CT scan, showed that the
bullet had gone through Malala's forehead but not her
brain. This was very, very good news. The doctors cleaned
and bandaged the wound, and Ziauddin waited with
unconscious Malala for her transfer via helicopter to
Lady Reading Hospital in Peshawar, where an excellent
neurosurgeon would be able to see her.

Meanwhile, Tor Pekai was worried and confused.
She had been at her first reading lesson when she
received word that Malala had been hurt, but the initial
news suggested that Malala had been in an accident
and hurt her foot. Tor Pekai rushed home to pray, but
it wasn't until Malala's brother, Atal, turned on the
television that she learned Malala had been shot in the
head. Tor Pekai longed to go to her daughter but was
told to stay home, as Malala was either dead or about to
be transferred to Peshawar.

At the sound of a helicopter overhead, Tor Pekai
rushed to the roof of the house, along with women who
had come to lend their support when they heard the news.
As the helicopter carrying her injured daughter flew over
the house, Tor Pekai did something extremely uncharac-
teristic: She removed her ever-present hijab, or head scarf.
She lifted it into the air, as if making an offering to God,
and cried, "God, I entrust her to You. We didn't accept
security guards—You are our protector. She was under
Your care and You are bound to give her back."

Combined Military Hospital in Peshawar

Ziauddin was surprised to find that Malala was *not* taken to Lady Reading Hospital, as they had been told. Rather, she was taken to the Combined Military Hospital (CMH), a large, 600-bed hospital that typically tended to wounded soldiers and those injured by suicide bombers. Ziauddin was leery of the hospital. Pakistanis tend to be distrustful of the military, who have seized power many times, and Swatis are especially wary of the military for waiting so long before taking action against the Taliban. Ziauddin would've preferred that Malala be at Lady Reading Hospital, but he didn't have any say in the matter.

Malala was taken to the intensive care unit, or ICU, where she was examined by the neurosurgeon on duty, Colonel Junaid Khan. By this time, Malala was conscious but not aware of her surroundings and not speaking. Colonel Khan located the bullet next to Malala's left shoulder blade, after noticing that there was no exit wound to match the entry wound. Based on the location of the bullet and the entry wound, Khan surmised that Malala must've been stooping forward with her neck bent when she was shot.

Khan also ordered another CT scan, and this time the news wasn't as promising. The CT done at Swat Central Hospital had been done from only one angle, but this new CT scan was more comprehensive. It showed that the bullet went very close to Malala's brain, and that particles of Malala's skull had damaged the brain membrane. The best course of action, he said, was to wait and see what happened.

Malala was beginning to give small indicators of responding. She was restless and grunting, trying to get the oxygen monitor off her finger, and whispering to those around her.

The hospital was four hours away, so Tor Pekai and Malala's brother Atal did not arrive until late that evening. Tor Pekai had been warned not to react too strongly to the sight of her wounded daughter, and she maintained her composure. But Atal was aghast at the sight of his injured sister, and he cried so hard that he had to be removed from her room.

Around midnight, Colonel Khan assessed Malala's condition again and reported to Ziauddin that her brain was now swelling dangerously. Malala was vomiting blood, fading out of consciousness, and beginning to deteriorate. They had to do surgery immediately to save her life. With shaking hands, Ziauddin signed the consent for surgery, which warned, "the patient may die."

Six hours later, the surgery was done. Colonel Khan removed an eight- to ten-centimeter square of Malala's skull and placed it inside the subcutaneous tissue in her abdomen to preserve it. The piece of skull needed to be removed to give the brain room to safely swell. While Malala was in the operating room, Khan performed a tracheotomy to relieve swelling that might block Malala's airway. He also removed blood clots from her brain, as well as the bullet from her shoulder blade. Malala was sent to recovery on a ventilator.

By the next morning, Malala had moved her arms, which was a good sign. However, three top surgeons who came to examine her suggested that she be put into a medically induced coma while she recovered, because there would be a lot of pressure on her brain if she regained consciousness.

By matter of coincidence, two British doctors happened to be in Pakistan the afternoon after Malala's surgery. The army chief, General Kayani, who had met Malala in 2009, asked them to stop by and assess her condition. Dr. Javid Kayani (no relation to General Kayani) was an emergency care consultant at Queen Elizabeth Hospital in Birmingham, England, and Dr. Fiona Reynolds was a specialist in children's intensive care from Birmingham Children's Hospital. These doctors from Birmingham were not pleased with the care Malala was receiving. Although they agreed that Colonel Junaid's operation had been life-saving, they weren't happy with the environment in which Malala would be recovering. Combined Military Hospital wasn't providing Malala with the around-the-clock monitoring she needed. Dr. Javid and Dr. Fiona, as Malala later called them, explained the monitoring Malala needed to be able to make the best possible recovery, and then they flew

The Taliban Response

The Taliban is well known for publicly taking credit for their attacks. It serves as an intimidation tactic, reminding people that the Taliban is in complete control and terrorizing them into submission. Interestingly, the Taliban was uncharacteristically silent on the assassination of Benazir Bhutto, leading many to question whether they were behind the attack. However, they were not silent about the attack on Malala. The Taliban issued a statement saying they had shot Malala, but they denied that it was because of her advocacy for education. Rather, they said:

> "We carried out this attack, and anybody who speaks against us will be attacked in the same way. Malala has been targeted because of her pioneer role in preaching secularism… She was young but she was promoting Western culture in Pashtun areas. She was pro-West; she was speaking against the Taliban; she was calling President Obama her idol."

Malala had indeed named President Obama as one of her favorite politicians, along with Khan Abdul Ghaffar Khan and Benazir Bhutto. This angered Fazlullah, who had ordered the attack on her two months prior to her shooting. A Taliban spokesman confirmed that the attackers were two Swati men who had purposely attacked the dyna near an army checkpoint to make the point that they could attack anywhere.

back out of Peshawar, where it was dangerous to be after dark. They reported to General Kayani that if Malala remained in Peshawar at Combined Military Hospital, she would suffer brain damage or die.

Two days after the assassination attempt, Malala's condition was continuing to deteriorate, and the hospital had made none of the changes in aftercare the doctors from Birmingham had recommended. Malala's vital signs weren't strong, her entire body was swollen, her kidneys and lungs were failing, and she was suffering from infection. Ziauddin was restless and distraught. Tor Pekai prayed ceaselessly.

Meanwhile, General Kayani sent two military intensive care specialists after receiving the negative report from Dr. Javid and Dr. Fiona. One of the specialists, Brigadier Aslam, reported to Dr. Fiona that Malala had developed disseminated intravascular coagulation, which means her blood was not clotting. Her blood pressure was very low, and the acid pH in her blood had risen. She was no longer producing any urine, resulting in kidney failure.

Dr. Fiona had been scheduled to fly back to Birmingham that day, but she changed her plans, returned to Peshawar, and helped arrange for Malala to be airlifted to the Armed Forces Institute of Cardiology in Rawalpindi, which had an excellent ICU.

Dr. Fiona was in her element as they flew to Rawalpindi, using all of the onboard equipment to monitor Malala's vital signs. She had spent her career working with critically ill children, and transporting them was nothing new for her. However, Malala's case was out of the ordinary for one simple reason: She had become a celebrity of sorts. Dr. Fiona later said,

> *"If anything had happened to her it would have been blamed on the white woman. If she'd died I would have killed Pakistan's Mother Teresa."*

Armed Forces Institute of Cardiology in Rawalpindi

It took three hours to stabilize Malala after they reached the Armed Forces Institute of Cardiology in Rawalpindi. She wasn't reacting well to the blood transfusions, but eventually Dr. Fiona and her team got Malala stabilized.

The hospital was on lockdown, with the strictest security measures in place to protect Malala and her family. Even the prime minister was denied entry when he went to visit Malala. No one underestimated the Taliban's ability to attack—they had already proven several times over that even highly guarded military establishments were not safe from their reach.

People around the world were outraged by the Taliban's brazen attack on Malala, but ironically, the

one place where Malala didn't have universal support
was Pakistan. Naturally, the Taliban felt their actions
were justified. But even some non-Taliban Pakistanis
felt negatively about Malala. Bloggers questioned
whether the shooting had even occurred, and conspiracy
theories abounded. Was Malala in cahoots with the
U.S. government? Was she really a CIA agent? Swatis
questioned what she had really done for the valley, feeling
that the praise and goodwill for Malala was unwarranted.
Others appeared to be jealous, complaining that the
publicity for Malala had overshadowed the good work
other Pakistanis had done for education.

Even though Malala lacked support from many
of her own countrymen, she certainly had a wealth of
international support. While she was in the Armed
Forces Institute of Cardiology, offers of help flooded in.
The Johns Hopkins Hospital offered her free treatment,
and American politicians John Kerry and Gabrielle
Giffords (herself a victim of a brutal shooting) offered
their assistance.

Interestingly, Ziauddin and Tor Pekai had very little
say in their daughter's treatment plan. General Kayani
made the decisions after consulting with Malala's
doctors, and his motives were at least partly political.
He hoped to build political support for an all-out
attack on the Taliban. As one of their most recognizable
and loved victims, Malala was a key part of the plan.
However, General Kayani was known to be kind and

compassionate, too, and had Malala's best interests at heart. She was not merely a pawn in a political game.

The ICU care at the Armed Forces Institute of Cardiology was solid and helped Malala stabilize from the devastating downturn her health had taken. However, Malala would need extensive rehabilitation to rebuild the strength in her arm and leg, as well as to combat a speech impediment related to the shooting. Pakistan did not offer such facilities, so Dr. Fiona suggested that Malala should be transferred out of Pakistan.

America was not a good option for Malala's rehabilitation, due to tensions between America and Pakistan. Instead, hospitals in London and Scotland were recommended. But General Kayani had other ideas. He wondered why Malala couldn't go to a hospital in Birmingham, England, where Dr. Fiona and Dr. Javid worked. After making a few calls, it was official: Malala would be transferred to Queen Elizabeth Hospital in Birmingham.

Queen Elizabeth Hospital in Birmingham

Transportation to Queen Elizabeth Hospital turned out to be a bit tricky. The Royal Air Force offered to transport Malala, but General Kayani refused—many conspiracy theories were already floating around about Malala, and he felt the presence of foreign military would only worsen things. The British government offered to help transport Malala, but they required a formal request from Pakistan, and the Pakistani government didn't want to sacrifice their pride by asking for help. Evidently, even a relatively simple patient transport wasn't immune to political implications!

Luckily, the head of the United Arab Emirates offered their private jet with an on-board hospital, and the General agreed that was a reasonable option. However, there was another hurdle to jump. Colonel Junaid informed Ziauddin that only he could accompany Malala to Birmingham; Tor Pekai, Khushal, and Atal would have to stay behind while a passport issue was sorted out. This, however, wasn't a reasonable solution— leaving Tor Pekai on her own with the two boys in Mingora presented a very real safety concern. Ziauddin refused to accompany Malala, stating that he had to stay with his family for their safety. But that decision, too, presented a problem—Malala was a minor and couldn't leave the country alone. So, Ziauddin signed documents to make Dr. Fiona Malala's legal guardian for the trip to the United Kingdom.

Finally, all of the bureaucracy was straightened out, and Malala was cleared to leave the country. Extreme security measures were in effect for her transport to the airport: The roads were shut down, and snipers were on the rooftops lining the route. Unfortunately, Malala was still unconscious and unable to enjoy the luxurious accommodations in which she was flown to the UK. The Emirates plane had sixteen first-class seats, as well as a mini-hospital attended by a German doctor and European nurses.

When Malala finally awoke from her medically induced coma the next day, she was in Queen Elizabeth Hospital in Birmingham, with no memory of her luxurious flight or the past several days in the hospitals. Malala recounts that her first thought upon regaining consciousness was, "Thank God I'm not dead." However, she had no idea where she was or where her parents were. The English-speaking nurses and doctors clued her in to the fact that she was no longer in Pakistan, as did the shiny, modern hospital, but she didn't know what country she was in. The breathing tube in her throat left

Queen Elizabeth Hospital in Birmingham, England.

her unable to speak, and the vision in her left eye was badly blurred.

The next day, when Malala was awake for longer periods of time, she tried to write down her father's phone number, but she was unable to write. Dr. Kayani brought her an alphabet board to point to letters, and she spelled out "father" and "country." A nurse told her that she was in Birmingham, England, but Malala still didn't know where her family was. Her head ached horribly, her vision was blurred, and she could feel that the left side of her face wasn't working properly—she couldn't hear out of her left ear, and the left side of her jaw wasn't moving correctly.

Finally, Dr. Fiona came in with a notebook and a pen for Malala, who this time was able to write the words, "Why have I no father?" and, "My father has no money. Who will pay for all this?" Dr. Fiona assured her that Ziauddin was safe in Pakistan and that Malala shouldn't worry about the money, but Malala *did* worry. Unaware of what a celebrity she had become, she had no idea that the Pakistani government was covering her medical bills and would ensure that her family was reunited. When she saw doctors speaking with each other, she assumed they were conferring about how her family would pay for her treatment. "I need to go out and start working so I can buy a phone and call my father so we can all be together again," she mused. She was consumed with worry about the medical bills and her family's safety in Pakistan. A call to her family, with the help of Dr. Javid, helped to reassure Malala, but she still worried.

As it turns out, she wasn't the only one worrying. Ziauddin and Tor Pekai had spoken to Malala by phone, but she hadn't been able to speak to them, as she still had a breathing tube in. Was Malala *really* okay, they wondered? They got conflicting reports from people who visited them—first they heard that Malala was doing well, and then they heard that her eyesight had been damaged and she couldn't see. It was a frustrating time for Ziauddin and Tor Pekai, who longed to be with their daughter but were stuck in Pakistan due to bureaucratic snags.

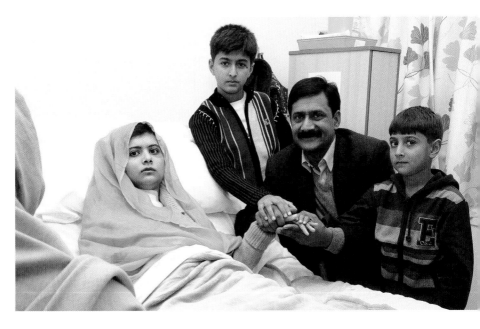

Atal (right), Ziauddin (center), and Khushal (left) visit Malala at Queen Elizabeth Hospital.

Meanwhile, in Birmingham, Malala was struggling to understand what had happened. Dr. Fiona told her that she had been shot on the school bus by the Taliban, and as Malala recalls, "My only regret was that I hadn't had a chance to speak to them before they shot me. Now they'd never hear what I had to say."

After a week at Queen Elizabeth Hospital, Malala's breathing tube was removed and she regained her voice, so she was able to speak to her father on the phone. Her family was still in Rawalpindi and had no idea when they would be coming to Birmingham. By then, Tor Pekai had had enough—she insisted that she would go on hunger strike if there was no news about their departure by the next day. That was the push it took to get things moving. Ziauddin reported Tor Pekai's threat to the major in charge of security, who promptly got the family moved to Islamabad, where the final paperwork could be taken care of.

It took several more days, but Malala's family finally left for Birmingham. By the time they reached their daughter, she had been in the hospital in Birmingham for ten whole days without them—ten days that felt like a hundred, as Malala recalls. It had been sixteen days since she was shot on the school bus. Sixteen days prior, she had been Malala, a Swati schoolgirl known reasonably well in Middle East advocacy circles. Now, she was Malala, "the girl shot by the Taliban," receiving cards and gifts from thousands of well-wishers around the world. She had become a global symbol for female rights in education.

Feminist advocates in Hong Kong tell Malala's story during a vigil for her in October 2012. After the assassination attempt, Malala quickly became a global icon for activism.

CHAPTER SIX

A Future for Advocacy

Birmingham, England, was a whole new world for Malala, who had never before left Pakistan and had rarely ventured out of the Swat Valley. Her first glimpses of England were from her hospital room, and she wondered where the mountains were. She marveled at the frequent mist and rain, and at the neat, orderly streets of red-brick houses, all looking exactly the same. It was a far cry from Mingora.

A Family Reunited

Malala was finally reunited with her family in her Birmingham hospital room sixteen days after she was shot, and she cried her first tears in sixteen days. She had remained stoic throughout her ordeal, but her emotion came pouring out upon seeing her family again.

Ziauddin and Tor Pekai were relieved to finally be reunited with Malala, but they were disturbed as well. Dr. Javid had warned them that Malala was only ten percent recovered and still had a long way to go, but they were not prepared to see the grimace that Malala wore when she tried to smile, due to damage to one of her facial nerves. Ziauddin said,

> *"The Taliban are very cruel. They have snatched her smile."*

Malala noticed that whenever she tried to smile, a shadow would pass over Tor Pekai's face. Malala's parents worried that in the future, the grimace would be a constant reminder of the shooting.

An Outpouring of Support

Malala was shocked at the incredible outpouring of support after the shooting. She received approximately 8,000 letters, many of them from schoolchildren. Many cards were simply addressed, "Malala, Birmingham Hospital," or even just "The Girl Shot in the Head, Birmingham." But that was all that was needed—everyone knew who Malala was, and the cards found their way to her.

In addition to the cards, Malala received teddy bears; chocolates; recognition from celebrities such as Beyoncé, Madonna, and Angelina Jolie; offers of adoption (despite the fact that her parents were still living); and even a marriage proposal. But most meaningful to her were two shawls that had belonged to Benazir Bhutto, which were sent by her children. Malala treasured the mementos from one of her idols.

Finding Malala's Attackers

During Malala's recovery, Ziauddin met with a group of politicians that included Rehman Malik, Pakistan's interior minister. Malik shared with Ziauddin that they had discovered the identity of Malala's attacker: He was a Talib named Ataullah Khan who had been arrested in 2009 but released after three months. Malik revealed that they had put a $1 million bounty on Khan's head, but Malala and her family knew the likelihood of his being caught was slim. After all, the Pakistani government hadn't caught any of the major assassins in recent history—not to mention they'd failed to catch Bin Laden, who had been hiding essentially in plain sight on Pakistani soil for years.

However, two people were arrested in connection with the assassination attempt: the driver of the dyna, Usman Bhai Jan, and the Khushal School accountant who had taken Usman Bhai Jan's frantic phone call the day of the shooting. The accountant was released after a few days, but Usman Bhai Jan was not because the army claimed they needed him to identify people. In other words, the innocent was in custody, but the assassin was not—much to Malala's despair. (As of August 2013, Usman Bhai Jan was still under house arrest, despite the fact that he is not a suspect in the shooting.)

Rehabilitation

At Queen Elizabeth Hospital, Malala continued her rehabilitation. On November 11, 2012, barely a month after the shooting, Malala underwent a major operation to repair the facial nerve in her face. Although a nerve sounds minor in the grand scheme of things, in reality this particular nerve helped to open and close Malala's left eye, raise her left eyebrow, move her nose, and make her smile. Repairing it was painstaking work, and the surgery lasted eight and a half hours. The surgeon found that two centimeters of the nerve were completely missing, and numerous bone fragments were restricting Malala's facial movement.

The surgery went well, and Malala was instructed to do facial exercises every day during her rehabilitation. After three months of this, the left side of Malala's face slowly began working again. Before long, she could smile once again and even wink her left eye. Although the surgeon had cautioned Malala that her face would never be completely the same again, he was delighted with Malala's progress, and declared the nerve eighty-six percent recovered—the best outcome he had seen in twenty years of doing facial nerve surgery.

Aside from the cosmetic success, the surgery brought another positive outcome: Malala finally got relief from the headaches that had been plaguing her since the shooting, and she was able to begin reading again. Furthermore, despite having no memory of the assassination attempt and frequently forgetting her friends' names, Malala's memory appeared to be improving.

Shortly thereafter, Malala had her first non-family visitor in the hospital: Asif Zardari, the president of Pakistan. Security was tight due to the media frenzy, and Malala recalls the visit being "like something out of a James Bond movie." President Zardari assured Malala that all her medical bills would be covered by the Pakistani government, and that he'd set up an apartment in Birmingham for Malala's family, so they would no longer have to live in a hostel. Perhaps most important, President Zardari gave Ziauddin a post as an education attaché, which provided Ziauddin with a salary and diplomatic passport. This ensured that the family would not need to seek asylum to stay in the UK.

A New Home

In early January, three months after she was shot, Malala was discharged from Queen Elizabeth Hospital and went to live in the Birmingham apartment with the rest of her family. Although she longed to return to Pakistan, there was no chance of it: The Taliban had made it known that they still intended to assassinate her. Setting foot back on Pakistani soil would be akin to signing her own death warrant, especially given that Maulana Fazlullah, who reportedly ordered the attack on Malala's life, now commanded the Taliban.

Birmingham was a very different world from Mingora. The family lived on the tenth floor of their apartment building, which was higher than they had ever lived, and Tor Pekai feared earthquakes, which were all too common in Pakistan.

The family lived in the center of Birmingham, and when Malala felt up to it, they took walks. Malala marveled at the coffeehouse in the square, where men and women could visit and chat with each other in a way that would've been strictly forbidden in Swat. They lived right near the famous Broad Street, which was filled with shops, bars, and strip clubs, and Malala, who was used to very modest clothing, was aghast at the skimpy clothing the women wore. If Malala was aghast, Tor Pekai was doubly so, and begged Ziauddin, "Please take me to Dubai. I can't live here!"

But live there they did, and they were even able to laugh about the situation. They had been warned not to go out on "dangerous" Broad Street at night. Given that the family was used to living in a town where the Taliban routinely beheaded people, it seemed utterly ridiculous to them to consider anything on Broad Street terribly dangerous!

Continued Rehabilitation

Malala was no longer in the hospital, but her recovery and rehabilitation were far from over. The missing piece of her skull was still safely in her abdomen, and she still had significant problems with her hearing.

In early February 2013, Malala went back into the hospital for another five-hour surgery. This time, two surgeons worked on her—one to replace the piece of her skull, and the other to insert a cochlear implant to resolve her hearing problems.

After retrieving it from Malala's abdomen, the first surgeon determined that the skull fragment had not kept well. Instead of using it and running the risk of infection, the surgeon placed a titanium plate with eight screws in Malala's skull. Thankfully, the placement of the cochlear implant went smoothly and without incident. When the external portion of the cochlear implant was fitted a few weeks later, Malala's hearing immediately started to improve.

Despite having essentially three surgeries in one day (one to retrieve the skull fragment from her abdomen, one to place the titanium plate in her skull, and one to place the cochlear implant), Malala recovered quickly and was back home in five days.

An International Ambassador

Nowadays, Malala is a teenager living in a small house in England, filled with her awards from countries around the world. She goes to school, having recovered enough by April 2013 to attend school in Birmingham. She enjoys her classes—despite having been placed two years behind where she was in Mingora, in order to help her prepare for the GCSE exams required of British students—and she is relieved to be going to school in a country where she doesn't have to fear a Taliban attack or a suicide bomber.

It sounds like paradise compared to where she came from, but Malala and her family are lonely. They miss their friends, family, and social life back in Swat. In England, they live alone, behind an iron gate that makes them feel as if they are on some sort of house arrest. They have privacy—but too much of it. They have a garden with plenty of room to play, but no one to play with. They have plenty to eat, but no one to share the leftovers with,

Malala addresses the United Nations at their headquarters in New York.

and Tor Pekai despairs about the waste of food. Malala has friends at school, but they are friends who see her as "Malala, girls' rights activist," rather than simply as Malala. According to Malala, "although I live in the West, I will always be proud to be a Muslim, a Pakistani, and a Pashtun. Wherever I am, I am still the same Malala."

Some people have accused the family of masterminding the entire attack—they suggest that the family wanted to leave Pakistan and found a way to do so. But the family dismisses such notions, pointing out that the family was happy in Mingora, and that Ziauddin had spent his life building his school and his reputation—things he would not willingly throw away to move to another continent.

Even as the family settles into their new life in Birmingham, Malala is aware that things will never be as they once were. She will never again be just a teenage girl. She has become a symbol for girls' education, for women's rights, and for international peace. And Malala takes her role as an international icon seriously, saying,

"I know God stopped me from going to the grave. It feels like this life is a second life. People prayed to God to spare me, and I was spared for a reason—to use my life for helping people."

The awards that line her family's living room remind Malala every day how much work still needs to be done for every boy and girl to receive the chance for an education. Malala has pledged to work tirelessly to advocate for this goal. On her sixteenth birthday, Malala addressed the United Nations in New York, calling on the audience to provide a free education to every child worldwide. "Let us pick up our books and our pens. They are our most powerful weapons. One child, one teacher, one book, and one pen can change the world," she said.

Despite the attempt on her life, Malala continues to advocate for a free education for every child worldwide.

The speech gained Malala supporters from all over the world—but not in her home country. Her fellow Pakistanis have accused her of using her advocacy and celebrity to get what they think she really wants—a life of luxury away from Pakistan. Malala vehemently denies the charge but harbors no ill will toward her countrymen, saying, "I know people say these things because they have seen leaders and politicians in our country who make promises they never keep... [T]hings in Pakistan are getting worse every day... People have lost trust in each other, but I would like everyone to know that I don't want support for myself, I want the support to be for my cause of peace and education." Malala also acknowledges that her detractors in Pakistan are fairly few—but they are "very active and very vocal."

Malala dreams of returning to Pakistan someday. But for now, she is aware that England is the best place for her—particularly as long as Fazlullah is head of the Taliban. It's safe, and the schools are good. A strong education will give Malala her "weapon of knowledge" to continue her advocacy for education rights. She remains in Birmingham, living a life of quiet (and sometimes lonely) strength. Someday, however, she hopes to return to her beloved Swat Valley and her Pashtun brothers and sisters.

2007

Pakistan Taliban launched; Benazir Bhutto returns to Pakistan after exile and is assassinated later the same year; Maulana Fazlullah sets up Islamic courts

July 12, 1997

Malala is born to father Ziauddin and mother Tor Pekai.

2004

First attack on Pakistan by a U.S. drone

Al Qaeda attacks the U.S. on September 11; U.S. War on Terror begins; Osama bin Laden escapes to Pakistan later that year

2001

Radio Mullah begins in Swat; massive earthquake strikes Pakistan and kills more than 70,000 people

2005

2012

Malala is shot in the head by the Taliban on October 9; she is briefly treated in Pakistan but later transferred to Birmingham, England, for rehabilitation

2010

Floods in Pakistan kill 2,000 people

Fazlullah announces all girls' schools in Swat will close on January 15; in January, Malala begins blogging for BBC Urdu as Gul Makai; also in January, Malala is filmed as the subject of the documentary *Class Dismissed in Swat Valley*; in February, Pakistani government and Taliban reach a peace deal; in April, the agreement breaks down and the Taliban takes over Swat; in May, the Pakistani army begins a military operation to drive the Taliban out of Swat, and Malala's family leaves Mingora on May 5; in July, the Taliban is declared cleared from Swat, and Malala's family returns home

2009

Osama bin Laden killed in Abbottabad, Pakistan; Malala wins Pakistan's National Peace Prize

2011

Malala is discharged from the hospital in January; in February, she returns for three more surgeries; in July, on her sixteenth birthday, she addresses the United Nations and calls for free education for all children; Malala is nominated for Nobel Peace Prize

2013

SOURCE NOTES

Chapter 1

P. 5, Malala Yousafzai with Christina Lamb. *I Am Malala: The Girl Who Stood Up for Education and Was Shot by the Taliban*. (New York: Little, Brown and Company, 2013), p. 309.

P. 6, "Pashtun." Encyclopedia Britannica Online. Retrieved January 23, 2014 from www.britannica.com/EBchecked/topic/445546/Pashtun

P. 7, Quoted in Yousafzai with Lamb, *I Am Malala: The Girl Who Stood Up for Education and Was Shot by the Taliban*, p. 14.

P. 7, Yousafzai with Lamb, *I Am Malala: The Girl Who Stood Up for Education and Was Shot by the Taliban*, p. 14.

P. 9, Quoted in Maria Rioumine and Adnan Rafiq. "Malala Yousafzai's Toughest Battle?" www.huffingtonpost.com, December 13, 2013.

P. 10, Husain, Mishal. "Malala: The girl who was shot for going to school." www.bbc.co.uk/news/magazine, October 7, 2013.

P. 11, Yousafzai with Lamb, *I Am Malala: The Girl Who Stood Up for Education and Was Shot by the Taliban*, p. 28.

P. 13, Yousafzai with Lamb, *I Am Malala: The Girl Who Stood Up for Education and Was Shot by the Taliban*, p. 17.

P. 17, Quoted in Yousafzai with Lamb, *I Am Malala: The Girl Who Stood Up for Education and Was Shot by the Taliban*, p. 56.

Chapter 2

P. 21, Yousafzai with Lamb, *I Am Malala: The Girl Who Stood Up for Education and Was Shot by the Taliban*, p. 111.

P. 22, Quoted in Yousafzai with Lamb, *I Am Malala: The Girl Who Stood Up for Education and Was Shot by the Taliban*, p. 112.

P. 24, Quoted in Yousafzai with Lamb, I Am Malala: The Girl Who Stood Up for Education and Was Shot by the Taliban, p. 115. (p19)

P. 25, Quoted in Yousafzai with Lamb, *I Am Malala: The Girl Who Stood Up for Education and Was Shot by the Taliban*, p. 125.

P. 28, Yousafzai with Lamb, *I Am Malala: The Girl Who Stood Up for Education and Was Shot by the Taliban*, p. 137.

P. 29, Quoted in Ellick and Ashraf, *Class Dismissed in Swat Valley*.

Chapter 3

P. 33, Yousafzai with Lamb, *I Am Malala: The Girl Who Stood Up for Education and Was Shot by the Taliban*, p. 124.

P. 33, Yousafzai with Lamb, *I Am Malala: The Girl Who Stood Up for Education and Was Shot by the Taliban*, p. 125.

P. 37, Yousafzai with Lamb, *I Am Malala: The Girl Who Stood Up for Education and Was Shot by the Taliban*, p. 139.

P. 38, Yousafzai with Lamb, *I Am Malala: The Girl Who Stood Up for Education and Was Shot by the Taliban*, p. 133.

P. 38, Yousafzai with Lamb, *I Am Malala: The Girl Who Stood Up for Education and Was Shot by the Taliban*, p. 141.

P. 38, Yousafzai with Lamb, *I Am Malala: The Girl Who Stood Up for Education and Was Shot by the Taliban*, pp. 141–142.

P. 39, Quoted in "Diary of a Pakistani Schoolgirl." news. bbc.co.uk, January 19, 2009.

P. 40, Yousafzai with Lamb, *I Am Malala: The Girl Who Stood Up for Education and Was Shot by the Taliban*, p. 157.

P. 40, Yousafzai with Lamb, *I Am Malala: The Girl Who Stood Up for Education and Was Shot by the Taliban*, p. 159.

P. 41, Quoted in Yousafzai with Lamb, *I Am Malala: The Girl Who Stood Up for Education and Was Shot by the Taliban*, pp. 168–169.

P. 42, Yousafzai with Lamb, *I Am Malala: The Girl Who Stood Up for Education and Was Shot by the Taliban*, p. 169.

P. 43, Quoted in Yousafzai with Lamb, *I Am Malala: The Girl Who Stood Up for Education and Was Shot by the Taliban*, p. 172.

P. 44, Quoted in Yousafzai with Lamb, *I Am Malala: The Girl Who Stood Up for Education and Was Shot by the Taliban*, p. 177.

P. 44, Yousafzai with Lamb, *I Am Malala: The Girl Who Stood Up for Education and Was Shot by the Taliban*, p. 179.

Chapter 4

P. 54, Yousafzai with Lamb, *I Am Malala: The Girl Who Stood Up for Education and Was Shot by the Taliban*, p. 215.

P. 55, Yousafzai with Lamb, *I Am Malala: The Girl Who Stood Up for Education and Was Shot by the Taliban*, p. 223.

P. 56, Yousafzai with Lamb, *I Am Malala: The Girl Who Stood Up for Education and Was Shot by the Taliban*, p. 224.

P. 56, Yousafzai with Lamb, *I Am Malala: The Girl Who Stood Up for Education and Was Shot by the Taliban*, p. 224–225.

P. 56, Yousafzai with Lamb, *I Am Malala: The Girl Who Stood Up for Education and Was Shot by the Taliban*, p. 225.

P. 57, Yousafzai with Lamb, *I Am Malala: The Girl Who Stood Up for Education and Was Shot by the Taliban*, p. 229.

P. 58, Yousafzai with Lamb, *I Am Malala: The Girl Who Stood Up for Education and Was Shot by the Taliban*, p. 237.

P. 59, Yousafzai with Lamb, *I Am Malala: The Girl Who Stood Up for Education and Was Shot by the Taliban*, p. 241.

P. 59, Yousafzai with Lamb, *I Am Malala: The Girl Who Stood Up for Education and Was Shot by the Taliban*, p. 241.

Chapter 5

P. 63, Quoted in Yousafzai with Lamb, *I Am Malala: The Girl Who Stood Up for Education and Was Shot by the Taliban*, p. 250.

P. 67, Quoted in Yousafzai with Lamb, *I Am Malala: The Girl Who Stood Up for Education and Was Shot by the Taliban*, p. 256.

P. 69, Quoted in Yousafzai with Lamb, *I Am Malala: The Girl Who Stood Up for Education and Was Shot by the Taliban*, p. 263.

P. 73, Salman Masood and Declan Walsh. "Pakistani Girl, a Global Heroine After an Attack, Has Critics at Home." www.nytimes.com, October 11, 2013.

P. 74, Yousafzai with Lamb, *I Am Malala: The Girl Who Stood Up for Education and Was Shot by the Taliban*, p. 275.

P. 74, Yousafzai with Lamb, *I Am Malala: The Girl Who Stood Up for Education and Was Shot by the Taliban*, p. 277.

P. 76, Yousafzai with Lamb, *I Am Malala: The Girl Who Stood Up for Education and Was Shot by the Taliban*, p. 278.

P. 76, Yousafzai with Lamb, *I Am Malala: The Girl Who Stood Up for Education and Was Shot by the Taliban*, p. 282.

Chapter 6

P. 80, Quoted in Yousafzai with Lamb, *I Am Malala: The Girl Who Stood Up for Education and Was Shot by the Taliban*, p. 292.

P. 80, Yousafzai with Lamb, *I Am Malala: The Girl Who Stood Up for Education and Was Shot by the Taliban*, p. 288.

P. 83, Yousafzai with Lamb, *I Am Malala: The Girl Who Stood Up for Education and Was Shot by the Taliban*, p. 297.

P. 84, Quoted in Yousafzai with Lamb, *I Am Malala: The Girl Who Stood Up for Education and Was Shot by the Taliban*, p. 299.

P. 87, Yousafzai with Lamb, *I Am Malala: The Girl Who Stood Up for Education and Was Shot by the Taliban*, p. 307.

P. 87, Quoted in Rioumine and Rafiq. "Malala Yousafzai's Toughest Battle?" par 2.

P. 88, Yousafzai with Lamb, *I Am Malala: The Girl Who Stood Up for Education and Was Shot by the Taliban*, p. 301.

P. 89, Yousafzai with Lamb, *I Am Malala: The Girl Who Stood Up for Education and Was Shot by the Taliban*, p. 310.

P. 89, Yousafzai with Lamb, *I Am Malala: The Girl Who Stood Up for Education and Was Shot by the Taliban*, pp. 310–311.

P. 89, Quoted in Yousafzai with Lamb, *I Am Malala: The Girl Who Stood Up for Education and Was Shot by the Taliban*, p. 311.

GLOSSARY

(ANP) Awami National Party, the Pashtun nationalist political party.

burqa A long garment, worn over regular clothing, that covers a woman's entire body. Some Pakistanis believe a burqa must be worn in public to preserve a woman's modesty. The burqa includes a rectangular face veil that is semi-transparent so the woman can see.

dyna An open-backed truck or bus.

jihadi A religious warrior.

madrasa An Islamic school.

mohalla Another term for district; a mohalla basically refers to a neighborhood or region.

mullah A Muslim educated in religious law and doctrine. Mullahs usually hold an official post.

Pashtun The Pashtun people live in northeastern Afghanistan and northern Pakistan, near the Hindu Kush mountains. The majority of the Afghan population is Pashtun, as are many of the people in the Swat Valley. At the turn of the twenty-first century, roughly eleven million Pashtun lived in Afghanistan and twenty-five million lived in Pakistan. The Pashtun are a patriarchal society based on Islam and Pashtunwali. Although hospitality and honor are of critical importance to Pashtuns, bloody feuds between families and clans are common.

princely state Princely states existed in India when it was under British rule. A princely state had a native ruler who had entered into a treaty with the British government. The Swat Valley, once part of India, was a princely state before it became part of what is now called Pakistan.

Quran Also spelled Koran or Qur'an. The main religious text of Islam. Muslims believe the Quran is a revelation from God to the prophet Muhammad.

shalwar kamiz Baggy pajama-type pants covered by a long tunic. Traditional dress of Pakistan for both men and women.

Sharia law Developed during the eighth and ninth centuries, sharia law upholds a system of beliefs governed by religious devotion. It governs personal law, including marriage, divorce, inheritance, and custody, as well as criminal law. The law is heavily open to interpretation, so offenses and punishments vary. However, depending on the interpretation, punishments for offenses can be severe and may include flogging, stoning, amputation, exile, and execution.

talib Originally, a religious student. In recent years, the term talib has come to refer to a member of the Taliban.

Taliban A militant Islamic fundamentalist group made up largely of Pashtuns.

TNSM TNSM stands for *Tehrik-e-Nifaz-e-Sharia-e-Mohammadi*, or the Movement for the Enforcement of Islamic Law. The movement was founded in

1992 by Sufi Mohammad. When Sufi Mohammad was imprisoned in 2002, his son-in-law Fazlullah took over as leader. He started an illegal radio station, Mullah FM, in a small village just outside Mingora. Fazlullah became known as Radio Mullah.

wali An Arabic term for a protector, guardian, or supporter. In the Swat region in the 1950s and 1960s, the wali was the head of state.

FURTHER INFORMATION

Books

Latifa. *My Forbidden Face: Growing Up Under the Taliban*. London, England: Virago. 2008.

Rowell, Rebecca. *Malala Yousafzai: Education Activist*. Minneapolis, MN: ABDO Publishing. 2013.

Yousafzai, Malala with Christina Lamb. *I Am Malala: The Girl Who Stood Up for Education and Was Shot by the Taliban*. New York, NY: Little, Brown and Company. 2013.

Websites

Council on Foreign Relations
Pakistan's New Generation of Terrorists
www.cfr.org/pakistan/pakistans-new-generation-terrorists/p15422
The Council on Foreign Relations maintains this site explaining the terrorist groups currently operating in Pakistan.

Malala Yousafzai
www.malala-yousafzai.com
This is a fan site dedicated to providing current news and information about Malala.

BBC News
Diary of a Pakistani Schoolgirl
news.bbc.co.uk/2/hi/south_asia/7834402.stm
This site includes several short, poignant entries from
Malala's diary as Gul Makai.

The World Factbook
https://www.cia.gov/library/publications/the-world-fact-
book/geos/pk.html
The CIA maintains this page providing general facts
about Pakistan.

Government of Pakistan
www.pakistan.gov.pk/gop/index.php?q=aHR0cDovLzE-
5Mi4xNjguNzAuMTM2L2dvcC8%3D
The government of Pakistan maintains this site providing
news and information about government, business, and
tourism in Pakistan.

Pakistan Higher Education System
www-db.in.tum.de/teaching/ws1112/hsufg/Taxila/Site/
Pakistan_UET.html
Created by a student at the University of Engineering
and Technology Taxila, this site provides information on
Pakistan's higher education system.

BIBLIOGRAPHY

Cahoon, Ben. "Princely States of India A–J." World-Statesmen.org. Retrieved January 23, 2014 from www.worldstatesmen.org/India_princes_A-J.html

"Diary of a Pakistani Schoolgirl." BBC News. news.bbc.co.uk/2/hi/south_asia/7834402.stm

Ellick, Adam B., and Ifran Ashraf. *Class Dismissed in Swat Valley.* www.nytimes.com, February 22, 2009. Retrieved on January 23, 2014 from www.nytimes.com/video/world/asia/1194838044017/class-dismissed-in-swat-valley.html

Ellick, Adam B., and Ifran Ashraf. *Class Dismissed: Malala's Story.* www.nytimes.com, October 9, 2012. Retrieved on January 23, 2014 from www.nytimes.com/video/world/asia/100000001835296/class-dismissed.html

Husain, Mishal. "Malala: The girl who was shot for going to school." www.bbc.co.uk/news/magazine, October 7, 2013. Retrieved January 31, 2014 from http://www.bbc.co.uk/news/magazine-24379018

Johnson, Toni, and Lauren Vriens. "Islam: Governing Under Sharia." www.cfr.com, January 9, 2013. Retrieved January 23, 2014 from www.cfr.org/religion/islam-governing-under-sharia/p8034

Koerner, Stephanie, and Ian Russell, eds. Unquiet Pasts: Risk Society, Lived Cultural Heritage, Re-designing Reflexivity. Farnham, Surrey, UK: Ashgate, 2010.

Masood, Salman and Declan Walsh. "Pakistani Girl, a Global Heroine After an Attack, Has Critics at Home." www.nytimes.com, October 11, 2013. Retrieved January 23, 2014 from www.nytimes.com/2013/10/12/world/asia/pakistanis-cant-decide-is-malala-yousafzai-a-heroine-or-western-stooge.html?_r=0

"Mullah." Merriam-Webster Online. Retrieved January 23, 2014 from www.merriam-webster.com/dictionary/mullah

"Pashtun." www.britannica.com. Retrieved January 23, 2014 from www.britannica.com/EBchecked/topic/445546/Pashtun

Rioumine, Maria and Adnan Rafiq. "Malala Yousafzai's Toughest Battle?" www.huffingtonpost.com, December 13, 2013. Retrieved January 23, 2014 from www.huffingtonpost.com/maria-rioumine-/malala-yousafzais-toughes_b_4435517.html

"Shari'ah." www.britannica.com. Retrieved January 23, 2014 from www.britannica.com/EBchecked/topic/538793/Shariah

"Wali: According to Quran and Sunnah." Muttaqun.com. Retrieved January 23, 2014 from muttaqun.com/wali.html

Yousafzai, Malala with Christina Lamb. *I Am Malala: The Girl Who Stood Up for Education and Was Shot by the Taliban*. New York, NY: Little, Brown and Company, 2013.

INDEX

ABOUT THE AUTHOR

Cathleen Small is a longtime editor and teacher who works primarily in the nonfiction field. She holds Bachelor's and Master's degrees in English, and specializes in substantive editing for nonfiction publishers. In addition, she teaches substantive editing for UC Berkeley Extension. A strong advocate in the Down Syndrome community, Cathleen was attracted to this project because of her desire to see advocacy in underrepresented populations. She resides in the San Francisco Bay Area with her husband and two young sons.